THE POWER OF LAUGHTER™

THE POWER OF LAUGHTER™

Seven Secrets
to
Living and Laughing
in a
Stressful World

by
Gail Hand

Published by:
The Power of Laughter™
3439 NE Sandy Blvd. #104
Portland, OR 97232
www.thepoweroflaughter.com

Oregon Editor: Marilyn McFarlane
Contributing Editors: Colleen Cady, Amy Anderson
                                    Gina Daggett
Copy Editor: Pat Skerrett
Photography: Dave Arpin, Portland
Design, Cover Art: Deb France

ISBN 0-9728783-0-0

Manufactured in the United States of America
First Edition

Special Thanks

To Deb France for her hard work on design, illustration, and continual love & support.

To my father Karl, my mother Audrey, my brothers Richard and Bruce, and all the animals we've loved. Thanks for the inspiration and the many giggles.

To Robin for your humor and creative mind.

To Rezan for everything a childhood friendship can bring to one's heart. Thank you for being.

Special thanks to Vicki, Suzan, Susy, Stephen, Sheryl, Sarah V, Roxanne, Ron, Roe, Patrick, Pat, Nancy, Marilyn, Lucy, Leonard, Lee, Janice, Jane, Hilary, Helene, Helen, Gina, Fred, Desi, Deanna, Dana, Cory, Cliff, Cathy, Brenda, Bea Audrey, Amy J.L., Amy A., and Allison for their inspiration, laughter, love, and input.

Special, Special thanks to Skip for your support, honesty, wit, and soul. Your talents are endless. Thank you for sharing them and always believing in me.

For Marcie, Scott, & Phil

Contents

Introduction 11

The First Secret
Laughter is very good for your health............ 15

The Second Secret
*Find the humor in your own family, very often
family members share a similar sense of
humor*.. 27

The Third Secret
Discover the joy in playing games 37

The Fourth Secret
*If you can think on your feet and keep
on laughing you will get through
the toughest of situations* 44

The Fifth Secret
*Humor can enrich your relationships and make
the unbearable, bearable* 61

The Sixth Secret
*Laughing can see you through- no matter what
circumstances life hands you* 71

The Seventh Secret
*Learning to cope with death is good for your
mental health and laughter can ease the pain* 84

Bibliography 95

Laughter Tools.................................... 97

Introduction

Laughter is a gift everyone should open.
--Gene Mitchener

Laughter gives us the opportunity to look at things from a different perspective. When faced with difficult or challenging situations I have always found laughter to be a huge stress relief. In my interviews with friends and acquaintances faced with personal or family illness, they concurred that the joy of having a laugh gave them a crucial break from the pain they were encountering. If you need some inspiration, don't miss the humor tools on pages 89 through 94.

The stories in the book are my personal experiences and those of close friends and family who have used laughter to get through difficult situations.

Each year, laughter is being taken more seriously as a healing tool in the medical field. More clinical studies are being shared internationally regarding the healing effects of laughter on the body. The studies found that patients who had a terminal or chronic illness improved their health by watching a series of humorous videos such as Laurel and Hardy, and Abbott and Costello. The children and adults had more pain free hours while watching the videos and it gave them a wonderful break from their situations.

In my research, I found it surprising that not a lot of work has been done in this field, however there is a name for the study, Geletology. (jel-uh-tall-uh-jee)

Many hospitals today have humor kits at their disposal, which they wheel around to patients in need of a fun break   These kits help patients to focus on something other than their illness, which often helps them to feel better. I will discuss the therapeutic benefits of laughter on physical, mental, and emotional well-being more in Chapter One.

For the past fourteen years I have been writing comedy to perform in clubs and venues across the country. In my travels I became a keen observer of all the events in life that were easy to laugh at. As we travel in our lives, things inevitably happen to take us off our chosen path. This often causes us to be less than pleased. My belief is that the stages of laughter are much like the stages of grief with a twist.

We need to go through the feelings of frustration, anger, denial and finally acceptance in order to get to the place where we can actually laugh. Some of us take more time than others. My path took me from years down to seconds, but it didn't happen overnight, and like many of us I had a lot of opportunities to practice the stages. The speed at which you go through the stages of getting to laughter is a learned trait. I wanted to share some of my personal trials over which I have prevailed, primarily due to my ability to use laughter as a survival tool. I have made a conscious decision to laugh on many occasions, especially when I was scared, anxious or even sad. This gift gave me the strength to get through some challenging emotional and physical situations over the years. More importantly, it gave me the ability to reflect on the ironies life handed my family.

Without laughter life would be difficult at best. My belief is that laughter is the antidote to most evils. No matter how hard life is, or how stressed you may be, eventually the power of laughter can prevail. It will help you heal from your woes and help you enjoy life more.

Enjoy!
Gail

ONE

The First Secret

Laughter is very good for your health

The power of laughter and humor is so profound there is a new segment of medicine called GELETOLOGY (jel-uh-tall-uh-jee) for its study. Geletology may sound like the study of gelatin, but it's not a sugar-coated type of dessert - it's low fat.

Dr. William Fry of Stanford University, a well known geletologist, noted that besides increasing heart rate and hormone production, laughter also improves muscle tone and circulation.

A hundred belly laughs is the aerobic equivalent of ten minutes on a rowing machine!

And you thought exercise wasn't fun!

Studies are being done today at UCLA's Johnson Comprehensive Cancer Center and Mattell USA Children's Hospital, with an endowment that Norman Cousins, a magazine editor, author and teacher at UCLA, left the school. These studies are showing the positive effects of humor on terminally ill children.
Groups are tested to see if I Love Lucy, Charlie Chaplin and Abbott & Costello videos will help improve their health. So far the studies are showing positive effects.

Laughter seems to induce a relaxation response in the part of the nervous system that controls involuntary functions of the body.
                    --Dr. Margaret Stuber- UCLA

Cousins wrote of his life-long experiment that if he laughed for twenty minutes without any reason, all his tensions would disappear. Cousins chronicled his use of laughter as a weapon in overcoming a terminal debilitating joint disease in his book, *Anatomy of an Illness.*

A big hearty belly laugh releases endorphins into the bloodstream. Seratonin is released into the body building up your psycho-neuro-immuological system. The vibrations from the laughter actually shake up and release the stress in our organs that have been rigidly holding all of your pent up emotions. So you see, laughter is essential for your biological health.

When was the last time you were laughing so hard at a joke you cried?

Wasn't that exhausting?

Remember how your stomach may have hurt, and you pleaded (doubling over with laughter), "No, stop- I can't laugh ANY more!"

Get it? Got it! Good.

Remember the Danny Kay movie, *The Court Jester?*
(Another movie guaranteed to make you laugh)

In our lives we have opportunities to laugh all day long. The question is how can we get to that place of acceptance and humor faster.
Are there any tips to remember?

First of all, I want you to know that as I wrote this section the fellow in front of me on my plane decided to put his seat back as far as possible, so that his head was in my lap. Frankly, as a writer I was very annoyed he would do this because it was hard for me to see my laptop's computer screen with the back of his seat pressing it into my lap. Once I got through my initial frustration and anger, I asked him if he was comfortable.
He said, "Yes, thank you for asking."
Now in some cases this fellow would detect the sarcasm in my voice and tell me about his right to plant his seat back into my lap and that I was supposed to just tough it out. Instead he sensed my lack of control in the situation as he had a right to recline his seat back and that was that.
Was I still angry? No, because I spoke my truth with my own non-attacking flair, giving me a chance to express my frustration and then I moved on. Was it an out-of-control, insane situation forcing me to look at his scalp for two hours?
Absolutely, yet I chose to fly to my destination and I cannot afford First Class at this point in my

career, therefore I must deal with the ever-present perils of riding coach.
I even offered him a blanket and some water.
In response we both laughed, and he went back to sleep in my lap. When we left the plane, I felt like I should have asked him his name, as I don't usually sleep with strangers.

Get it now? You've got it! Good.

Think of a situation where you lost your cool and wish you hadn't.
Rewrite that scenario in a humorous way.

Doesn't that feel a lot better?

I often write letters to customer service agents and delete them. They annoy me the most in my daily life. Especially the ones that put you on hold to get advice from a supervisor and come back saying that they still cannot help you. When we need technical support with computer software or hardware for instance, we become dependent on the expertise of others –an often precarious position with varied response. Our only choice is how we react – either with a sense of humor or a major headache.

The Weekend Retreat

One weekend, I went skiing with two older friends up in Lake Tahoe. Both were in the field of psychotherapy; one is now head of an entire graduate program. We were in one of those silly moods that friends can get into when they're alone in the woods in a cabin with no one to witness the level of their childish antics.

The marshmallow roast started out innocently enough. Then the marshmallow fight began! It escalated to a full-scale marshmallow attack, with two against one. Finally, we barred ourselves behind doors, using decorative wooden geese to knock on the doors. As soon as the unsuspecting one would open the door, she would see a goose, with marshmallows strewn behind it, and begin laughing again. At which point, the other two would bombard her with more marshmallows. This went on for at least 20 minutes, and was one of the best laughs I have had in my life.

Hey, that's great, but what does this have to do with the power of laughter?

The news here is that one of my friends had a sister who was just diagnosed with breast cancer, and the other was going through a divorce while I was struggling with my grades in college.
We found a way to lighten our loads, if only for a few minutes.

Last month I saw both of these friends at the wedding of one of their daughters. We recalled our memorable marshmallow weekend of fifteen years ago. We all started laughing immediately, as though it were yesterday.

We created a powerful memory by being completely silly during a break from our own individual tragedies. It had left us refreshed and ready to face the world.

Take a moment now and think of an enjoyable event that you've been reminiscing about while reading this story. Were you going through anything at the time that was stressful? Perhaps it was divorce, death in the family, illness, moving, money issues, work issues, school issues, or an auto accident? Chances are that you, or one of your relatives involved, was going through such an event and that moment of laughter was *vital* to that person's ability to cope during that difficult time.

I am also an advocate of therapy, bodywork and many forms of spirituality. All of these lead to the release of sadness, anger and, eventually, the laughter we carry inside. As we peel away the layers of emotions, humor and perspective get an opportunity to emerge, and to cheer us - even if it is only for a brief moment.

In my case, laughter was both my coping mechanism and the tool I used in therapy to get to my true feelings. The laughter was very useful and eventually took me to a "lighter place."

Getting to that lighter place many of us seek is sure to reduce our stress levels. Why do you think there are almost as many Yoga studios in some towns as coffee shops? A trend? Perhaps.

Two rules for stress management: "Rule one: Don't sweat the small stuff. Rule two: It's all small stuff.

--Robert Elliot

The Taoists are even more specific:

My barn having burned to the ground, I can now see the moon.

--Taoist saying

Laughter boosts the immune system, improves blood circulation, lowers blood pressure, makes your heart stronger, reduces stress and stimulates the nervous system.

Yoga

If you have ever had the chance to take a Yoga class, you will be able to relate to this piece.

My spine is fused as a result of spinal surgery to repair Scoliosis I had developed as a teenager. For fifteen years I enjoyed competing in eight different sports competitively. The sixteenth year my back became tired and I developed a very bad case of arthritis. Living in San Francisco, many of my friends tried to talk me into taking Yoga to help my back. Finally one year I had the courage to go with a friend who had severe knee problems after having surgery several years prior.
We got to class, and I walked right up to the instructor to tell him about my rod. He said something I will never forget:
"I've broken every bone in my body from riding a motorcycle, this will not only help you- it will get rid of all the crap inside your back you are holding onto."
Not only was he the was the best Yoga teacher I ever had, he pushed me further than I ever thought I could go. The beauty of this is that while feeling every muscle in my body, I was laughing at the absurdity of the positions we were doing. The poses even have funny names:
Corpse Pose, Downward facing Dog.

Yes a dog faces downward naturally, what else do we learn to do in this position I pondered?

The *Corpse pose*, why do we need to practice this at all? When we are dead, isn't the corpse pose a natural phenomenon for us?

The Corpse pose happens to be my favorite, hence my secret love of gallows humor.

Most of my yoga classmates were very serious. It was hard to ignore all the moaning and groaning from the rest of the class and focus on my own goal to hold these poses. I would stretch as far as I could and I looked pathetic compared to my neighbor. So I would look at my friend Abbe, make a funny face and start laughing. Then she would start laughing. We often had to be separated because then several others in the class started to laugh. Nonetheless, it was a great release and I found that the more I laughed the better my stretching became. All of a sudden I was having fun instead of "exercising".

The joy of yoga is not only in the absurdity of the poses, it's in the peace, breath and joy that they bring to your body as a result of a good yoga practice.

After moving away from San Francisco, I have yet to find a teacher as great as Joe. Instead I practice at home with my dogs. They do the most authentic *downward dog* you have every seen.

This way I laugh while I do yoga, which I call "doga". I'm sure this is frowned upon by the Yogi Masters in India, but I got the idea from the Yoga Journal and just expanded on it.

24

For those who suffer from allergies

A recent study was done on patients who were allergic to dust mites, cedar pollen, or cat dander in Japan. They were not given any medication for 72 hours prior to the test. They were then shown a humorous 87-minute video and then retested. The symptoms of the patients were significantly reduced for the next four hours.

After watching a weather video the patients were tested again no improvement was shown.

Obviously we need more funny weather people.

A last note on Laughter and the Body

Extensive scientific research shows that:

Laughter reduces serum cortical.
(a hormone released during the stress
response)

Laughter increases immunoglobin A.
(an antibody that helps fight upper
respiratory disease)

Laughter increases tolerance to pain.

Laughter increases the heart rate, pulse rate and
juggles the internal organs.

Almost everyone knows someone who is battling
some form of cancer. The people I interviewed
for this book who have encountered cancer in
their lives have all told me that their health is
directly related to their laughter quotient.

If we can offer comfort and humor to someone
who is ill, we can actually help them feel better,
even if for a short time.
True support doesn't get much better than that.

TWO

The Second Secret

Find the humor in your own family, very often family members share your similar sense of humor

Humor is an attitude. It's a way of looking at life and of telling others how you feel about what's happening around you.

--Gene Perret

As we all know too well we can't choose our relatives, but we *can* choose to laugh at ourselves when we instinctively mimic our mother's nasty habit of putting a used tissue up her sleeve when we have a cold. Or when we lose our glasses in the house twelve times in a week. Your family and your role in it is an endless source of comedy in it's purest form.

A great movie to illustrate this universal family dynamic is *Home for the Holidays.* Everyone can find something they can relate to and reminds them of their own family.

Talking to the Wall

My family grew up about an hour outside of
Manhattan. Some of my favorite memories of
laughter were while visiting my grandparents
in the Bronx. In fact we would sing that famous
song on the way: "Over the river and through the
woods to grandma's house we go".
And then we would laugh because no one
remembered the next line.

Since my father was always grandma's little boy,
she treated him like a child so even as an adult, he
would have to fight for respect at times.

Sometimes my father would come over to the
house and try to talk to my grandmother about
a suggestion he had for fixing something or
improving something in her house, and Grandma
would just tune him out.
He would then turn to the wall and start talking to
the wall.

Grandma: *Karl, what are you doing?*
Karl: *I am talking to this wall because talking to
the wall is like talking to you only the wall may
listen to me!*

We would all start laughing, and then grandma
paid attention. Dad got a reaction and we all got
huge entertainment value.

My grandparents had a unique style of couples communication, which still makes me laugh when I think about it.

Grandpa was hard of hearing, and would often forget to turn up his hearing aid. We were all convinced he turned it down so he wouldn't have to listen to Grandma nag at him.

Grandma:	*Dave, are you sleeping?*
Grandpa:	*Vat ?*
Grandma:	*Are you sleeping?*
Grandpa:	*Huh?*
Grandma:	*Dave, are you hungry- I'll make you some liver!*
Grandpa:	*I'm hungry, what are you making?*

This back-and-forth would continue until he heard a "food" word, and then suddenly he would get up out of his recliner and shuffle over to the table to eat.

Grandpa had a glass of "schnapps" with his meal every day. We were all convinced that is why he lived until he was 97. That and his sly sense of humor.

Lights Out

My grandmother came to stay with us in California when I was a teenager. She and Grandpa were sleeping in my dad's office in the guest beds. There was a bathroom on the same floor. I had come home from a date and turned the lights off, as I was always instructed to do, if I was the last one home.

Some time later my grandmother got up to go to the bathroom, which was 15 steps from her bed. She got disoriented, however, and walked in the opposite direction out the door and fell down the carpeted flight of five steps. I was sound asleep during all of this and awoke when they returned from the hospital emergency room. All I heard was: "We were in the emergency room all night. Everyone's fine, go back to sleep."

I went back to sleep, thinking nothing big had happened. In the morning I marched downstairs to have breakfast. As I reached the bottom stair I heard my grandmother yell, "Why did you try to kill me?" I looked up to find my grandmother sitting at the kitchen table with her head bandaged like a soldier and her arm in a sling. She screamed at me as my mouth dropped open.

Grandma: *Did you turn out the light last night?*

Me: *Uh-huh.*

Grandma: *Oh never mind that...what time did you get home?*

She was in pain, but she smiled at me and winked.

Grandma: *So what time **did** you get in, and WHY did you turn out the light?*

Me: *I turned out the lights because YOUR SON has instructed us to turn them out, because they waste electricity!*

Grandma didn't miss a beat and blurted:

Karl, you care more about the electricity bill than my health?

Relatives always have a way of amusing us no matter what the circumstance.

A conversation with Grandma

What's that Grandma? You made some **chopped liver?** Oh, I can have some, but don't tell my brothers? Oh, OK, I think I can make the same fork mark in it that you did and still get a bite.

Lottie outfitted for Halloween

What? **Cantaloupe too**, wow, you must really love me, you know how I love cantaloupe. Oh, the garbage, sure I'll take it out. The light bulb is out? Yes, I'll get the spares in the linen closet...it would be my pleasure. **Lemon drops?** No, Mommy will find out I got away with murder if I eat those, I'll be too full for the soup. Yes, I know you made my favorite **knadles**, I have to save room for them so no lemon drops.

Owwww Grandma you always squeeze my cheeks so tight. Are you going to change out of your housedress today for dinner? Oh, you were cooking so you didn't want to soil your blouse, I understand. Yes, I know I'm your baby granddaughter; you tell me that every time you squeeze my cheeks. **Casino?** OK but can we play for something other than pennies? Raisins,

33

yeah that would be fun, especially on the ride home in the car with my brothers.

Where's Grandpa? Oh yeah, it's Saturday. Will he be back from Temple soon? How far is it anyway, only two blocks? Why does he need to pray for so long? Are you sure he's not really in the park playing pinochle with his friends?

Grandma, will you sing to me again? I love it when you sing. Didn't you used to be in the opera? I think I inherited your genes. Except for that nose, my nose isn't that big. I definitely have your hands- see? It's your turn to discard. Grandma, are you sure you want to throw that card out? OK, I win.

I'll go set the table, **no I can't eat any more cantaloupe** I will get discovered because my belly will burst. What did you say? Oh, thank you, Grandma I will spend it wisely, I promise. No, I won't tell my brothers. It's just between us girls. Grandma I told you I like boys, I just am very picky that's all. **Oh, you and Sylvia were the Lesbians of Allerton Avenue?** You used to kiss on the lips all the time? That's interesting.

Grandma, this is Joanna, she is my roommate. **No she doesn't have a boyfriend either,** and we go to college together at F.I.T. No, she's not Jewish she's Italian. Yes I agree the Jews and the Italians both like close families. OK, so she's now an official honorary Jew. Isn't that great, Jo? Joanna, **do you want some gefilte fish?** Grandma made it fresh today. You love gefilte fish? You are scoring big points with Grandma. Do you play cards? **Grandma, don't squeeze Joanna's cheeks**. Oh, you're used to it because your Grandma did the same thing? I see. Bowling? You bowl here at the center, that's cool.The seniors are cheering for you Grandma. **"Lottie, Lottie, shake."**

Grandma I can't move my hips like that, are you sure we are related? Ever thought about trying out for the Rockettes? Yes, I know you can dance just like them. Be careful Grandma, I want you to save some energy for our walk home. Oh, you want me to be married and *then* have a child? **$5,000 if I get a boyfriend, I see. How about $1,500 for a butch with a mustache?** Grandma, don't be upset, I am much happier with women. I'm glad that you still love me, and yes, mom and dad know. Well, they are not ecstatic but they are accepting it. Yes, I may like to have children someday. **I know I need a man to have children, but they have things called sperm banks now.**

Grandma stop screaming so loudly, the neighbors will think you are getting mugged. Thank you for trying to understand. No, it's inseminate not instigate. **I love you too, Grandma.** Can we play some Casino now? OK, pennies would be good; I need to save for the sperm bank so you can get a great-grandchild out of me like you wanted. That's plenty for **carfare,** grandma. I only took the subway! Okay, thank you I'll buy you some flowers next visit. No, you deal...

Lottie Hand 1904-1995

Nicknames

To this day I have found one good use for geometry, and that is billiards. We started playing pool when I was five. It was a huge source of entertainment and a great opportunity for family bonding.

Dad used to call me "Eagle Eye Fleagle." In fact he had names for all of us. My eldest brother was "Rasputen J Mulvaney;" the other, "JR Fafoofnakoff." As for me, when I walked down the stairs in the morning he would sing, "Here she comes, Miss America," and I would giggle, knowing I was daddy's little girl. My mother had the foreign version; she was, "Chaumont, Chaumont, Chaumont." (French for how lovely, three times) We tried very hard to come up with a name for Dad. The best we could do was, "JJ Daddy." Hey, we were little kids!

My grandmother called me "Sugar puss" while I was growing up. It was fine when I was a kid. As I got older, it became a little embarrassing, especially on the few occasions when we went shopping together. Humiliation was a mild word for what I felt at age 14, when she would yell from one aisle to the other, "Sugar puss", they have the Coco Puffs you're always sneaking up to your room."
Now that Grandma is not around to call me by this name, my father has taken on the tradition, only he has shortened it to "puss."

Our family showed us the true value of being playful and laughing with children.

THREE

The Third Secret

Discover the joy in playing games

To play is to yield oneself to a kind of magic
-- Hugo Rahner

My mother recently read an obituary that was in her local paper. Inserted was a strong list of the deceased attributes. It read:
"He loved to cheat at Pinochle."

Playing games is an essential way to bring peoples hidden strengths and weaknesses to the surface. Rules are stretched, twisted and broken in order to accentuate ones creativity. Winning and losing both have it's advantages, but the playing of the game is what can bring you the most joy.

This applies particularly well to dating.

Michigan Rummy

We played Michigan Rummy with my grandparents at our house after most holiday meals. Michigan Rummy is a simple game where you put chips on to what are called "money cards" in the middle of the table on a rubber mat that shows what the money card is. You run through a suit of cards by playing them in order from lowest to highest and if you get to play a money card, this allows you to pick up money in the pot.

The strategy: Pay attention to what card is being played. When it is your turn, you start with the lowest card in a particular suit in your hand, and put it down. The next person who has a higher card in that same suit puts down a card and so it continues. Not too difficult to master, right? (ie. 2,3,4) Then there was my family…

My eldest brother, who was bi-polar and heavily medicated, (but high functioning) would put down whatever card he felt like every so often. This cracked us up, because he did it unpredictably. He was also tricky because he would win half the time.

Then we had my grandfather, who was in his 80's and couldn't hear very well. We had to wake him up occasionally because he would doze off.

My grandmother would hardly be paying attention. Thus my other brother would lean over and look at her cards every five minutes, to make her laugh. These game delays would spur my father to yell at all of us (in his sweetest voice), to "PLAY!"

This is one of my fondest childhood memories, and it always makes me smile. When I am having a difficult day, I think of Michigan Rummy. I think we played it more for the entertainment factor than the game itself.

Did I mention we played for real money?

Take a minute to think of one of your most enjoyable childhood memories.

Smile at each other; smile at your wife, smile at your husband, smile at your children, smile at each other- it doesn't matter who it is- and that will help you to grow up in greater love for each other.

--Mother Teresa

In our family, games were a welcome respite almost every Saturday night. Since we were young, our parents got us together to learn about games, the joys and the pitfalls of using different strategies. On those nights and rainy afternoons we got to know each others character. Learning the way each other would react to winning or losing, or better yet, almost winning or losing.

Parchese

My eldest brother is bi-polar and clinically medicated for manic depression. He has always been very high functioning and an extremely covert strategist at several games. He loved playing Racko, Stratego, and Parchese.
He was particularly devilish at Parchese. His signature move would be to form a blockade with his playing pieces to keep everyone on the board from progressing. The best part was that he smiled when he did this and watched us all squirm for what seemed like days with his strategy. Looking back fondly I find myself giggling at his mastery of a game that no one thought he understood.

Genius works all around us.

The Elusive Marvin Gardens

My friends had heard stories from other kids in the neighborhood about what it was like to participate in game night in the Hand household. They had theories and sometimes professed an interest in participating.

One night, my best friend Marci came over to play Monopoly with our family. My father had a little temper problem, along with his raging competitiveness. Little did he know, however, that Marci was quite familiar with this behavior from her own father. It is funny what you can get away with, with other people's parents that you can't with your own.

My father wanted to trade some yellow properties with Marci. Despite the 25-year age difference, she was smart enough to know it was not advantageous for her or the rest of us to trade with him, even though she was losing and he offered generous cash rewards. She tortured my father by not cooperating, which of course kept us all in hysterics because this 16- year old girl was making my father crazy by refusing to play by his rules. The rest of the family just went about our business in helping each other trade amongst ourselves while they duked it out.

We were all laughing the whole time during the exchanges. In the end, my father had a temper tantrum and left the table.

The remaining group all shook our heads, re-dispersed his properties and went on with the game. We laughed at the magic of it all when, in the end, Marci won.

It might have seemed as though she had the worst strategy in the game but she ended up winning! Why? Because she refused to give up her ground and smiled at my father while she did it. He couldn't stand it and he quit. Mind you, my father has a very good sense of humor, he is just a bear to play Monopoly with. As soon as he would lose his temper, we all would break into laughter because we knew it was just a game, like life. The pleasure you derive from it is all in how you choose to play.

You may be getting an idea after these few examples of how you can apply this attitude towards your present problem, difficult situation or family member.

When in a situation where you are dealt a lousy hand and you want to win or lose gracefully you need to use a different strategy.

Hold your ground, play a good defense and keep your sense of humor. It drives others crazy.

My favorite game these days is *Cranium.* Players team up and have a choice to do impersonations for their teammates, play with clay, draw with their eyes close, or hum a tune while others try to guess what it is. It's great fun and laughter is guaranteed!

However, please note for future reference- I am not very good at humming.

Improvisational Comedy

The first time I discovered improvisational comedy, a friend dragged me to a show. I had no idea what would happen when I got there, and luckily I was pleasantly surprised with the outcome. San Francisco is the home to BATS Better known as *Bay Area Theater Sports*.

The shows were wildly entertaining, so much so that I signed up for one of their workshops and have been forever hooked. I find improvisation an important part of many business situations, personal situations in and outside of work and a general survival tool for all mortal citizens.

The goal of improvisational exercises is to generate camaraderie, trust, and joi de vive between the participants. This allows people to get in the moment and be prepared to take risks with the other players that they are about improvise with. Most of them are down right goofy, and would be equally good ice- breakers at a party or welcome week on a school campus or at a company workshop.

You can discover more about a person in an hour of play than in a year of conversation
                                                    --Plato

FOUR

The Fourth Secret

If you can think on your feet and keep on laughing you will get through the toughest times

In the late 1850s, Abraham Lincoln was challenged to a duel. He said, "I accept if I can specify the weapons and the distance at which we stand." The other man agreed. Lincoln said, "Cow shit at five paces." End of fight.

While I was growing up in New York, we had a lot of thunderstorms. At first my brothers and I would get very scared as did our dog, Charlie Brown. My mom decided she would make the event enjoyable instead. As soon as we heard the first boom, she would beckon us to help her make some hot chocolate in the kitchen. Once it was done, we would all sit together by the enormous living room window and drink hot chocolate with marshmallows. We would count the seconds between the thunder and lightning to try and figure out how far away the storm was.

Instead of screaming with fear, we laughed with excitement.

Mom receives ten points for creative problem solving!

Subway Screamer

It's 1959. There's a smartly dressed woman standing amidst a jam packed, rush-hour crowd full of New Yorkers.
Her subway car is filled with mostly men standing body to body; there is barely enough room to grab a handle as the train ramble through the East Side.

Suddenly she feels someone run a hand up her backside. Knowing this is a man taking advantage of her amidst a crowd of strangers, my mother screams at the top of her lungs,

"Would you mind scratching a little bit higher?"

Within a blink of an eye, all the men move to the outside of the subway car and the women flock to my mother. They smile silently for the rest of the ride.

*This story was told to me over and over by my mother to remind me to speak up for myself when I am feeling cornered or taken advantage of. She taught me I could even do it **with** a sense of humor. We are never victims in this life if we choose to fight.*
*Find your voice and your humor--they **can** co-exist!*

Cherishing this example my mother taught me, I too had a few memorable times that defined my inner power of action with a smile.

Fashion puppies unite

The year is 1980. I am getting off BART in San Francisco with my schoolmates from the Fashion Institute of Design & Merchandising.
We all proceed across the street into the building next door. Giggling, we nod at the security guard at the front door and board the elevator together.
There are four of us on the elevator and as the doors are closing, a man dressed in a raincoat jumps in with us.
The doors close and the odor is horrible. We all move as far away from him as we can, at which point he moves to the rear of the elevator and starts harassing one of the other girls. I hit the emergency call button, and punch all the floors on the elevator before anyone can blink an eye. I am laughing and they are screaming, because I have confidence the guy is not armed and we will get out of the situation shortly. When we get to the second floor, a crowd of people including the lax security guard waiting for us to see what all the commotion is about.

Everyone steps aside as the other three girls run screaming out of the elevator. The man then has the audacity to try and move to me as the girls were running out in a flurry. I elbow the guy and shove him so hard to the back of the elevator that there is a loud thud.

He is so shocked he runs out of the elevator with the rest of the group and tries to exit the building right by security guy, who catches him on the way out.

Fashion Maidens - 1   Flasher – 0

When I told this story to the President of the College, I was furious about the security guard not doing his job. The President and I both started to laugh at the same time, knowing I probably injured the flasher pretty handily and may want to apply for the job myself.

Life can be wildly tragic at times, and I've had my share. But whatever happens to you, you have to keep a slightly comic attitude. In the final analysis, you have got not to forget to laugh.
                                        --Katherine Hepburn

October 17, 1989
Claremont Hotel, Berkeley, California.

I'm working for Brady Marketing in the San Francisco Bay Area as a manufacturer's rep for gourmet houseware products. Macy's entire houseware staff from the Bay Area stores is on their way for a training session our company is about to conduct. I take a quick trip to the bathroom to change into a skirt. If you have ever seen the *Poseidon Adventure*, this was the scene that was cut out and left on the editing room floor. The bathroom stall started to move; I thought someone was having a good laugh on my time. The ceiling started to flake apart above my head. It was at this point I knew I was alone in an old hotel with my skirt around my ankles in the middle of an earthquake. I pulled up my skirt, managed to get the door to the stall open when more of the ceiling started to fall onto the floor. I remembered that they taught us in school to stand in the doorjamb. Opening the door, I took my first breath as I watched a man running up the stairs towards me. I yelled, "Don't look, I'm not dressed!" He yelled back, "Lady, I don't care what you look like, we're having an earthquake and I just want to get out of here alive!" At that point I laughed and turned to my right to see my boss Stuart standing in the men's doorway holding his pants. He was as white as a ghost. He looked at me and said, "Is it my fault?"

About a minute later when we all gathered in the ballroom to see if everyone was accounted for there was a lot of whispering going on. The next thing you know, my friends from work carried out a beautiful homemade birthday cake for me as a surprise.

I'll never forget that birthday!

We all were stressed beyond belief but they thought it fitting to **still** celebrate my birthday; it was the sweetest song I ever heard.

You increase your joy by increasing the pure joy of others.

--Torkom Saraydarian

When we all returned to the office that next week, the office staff made a point to dive under their desks when my boss neared the bathroom. They all would yell, "Hit the deck, Stuart's going to the bathroom, an earthquake is sure to follow."

Just in case it was his fault, they wanted to be prepared.

Software for a Song

I have found that with a sense of humor it is still easy to remain professional when dealing with a difficult work issue. It lightens everyone's mood and helps the task at hand go more smoothly. One of my favorite work stories is about new software we got at a Fortune 500 Company where I enjoyed working for several years. The software had so many bugs in it that the spiders in my house were jealous. A friend of mine was the regional support person for this new product; she played the liaison between the software back-up support and the field of helpless salespeople.

I got the software engineer's cell phone number and, after a week I was forbidden to call him. Even though I tried to make him laugh when I spoke to him, he was a serious engineer who felt his ego was getting bashed.
I laughed it off and proceeded to forge an even stronger relationship with our regional rep. So she wouldn't cringe every time I called, I decided to make her laugh.

Every time I had a problem, which was every other day, I would call and *sing* to her. I sang loudly and changed the song each day; I just made the songs up. She liked it so much, we became great friends and now I talk to her every day.

Had I just treated the problems like headaches, we never would have become such good friends and, I wouldn't have had a chance to practice my operatic tunes.

Travels with George

My philosophy in life is to try and discover what it is you are meant to do here on the planet, then learn how to have fun doing it.

I discovered many years ago that one of my special gifts was the ability to make people laugh. Remaining a kid at heart, I have continued my obsession with Curious George that began when I was a very small child. Now that my profession is to entertain others, I travel often with my furry companion, Curious George the puppet.

Our adventures together began the morning I ran into a famous movie star in the Red Carpet club at Los Angeles International Airport.

The movie star was in a particularly gnarly mood and it did not help that I apparently stole her phone. I saw a Diet Coke sitting on the table in front of a phone. There with no warm body attached to it, so George and I proceeded to use the phone. She glared at me upon her return to her soda and shouted, "She **STOLE** my phone!" I ignored her outburst and finished my call, then watched her scream at the manager who had neglected to send anyone to meet her at the airport.

The poor fellow was trying to receive sympathy from **'old Mummy Dearest'....**I just had to laugh. The phrase "you can't squeeze blood from a turnip" came to mind. I felt like saying to her,

"Hey famous movie star, know what I have in my bag? Wire Hangers!" In reality, I waited a few minutes and looked at her and said:

"Don't you just hate incompetence?" To which she replied staring over her bifocals at me: **"I REALLY have no time for it!"** Then she glared at my monkey, rolled her eyes and went back to hiding behind her New York Times. What a great start to our trip!

Moving on to Vegas.... I was reeling from having a bit of a confrontation with Faye that morning, so by dinner I was quite punchy. That was when **I decided to take George gambling with me.**

We sat down at the blackjack table and I put him on my hand after receiving our first two cards, determined not to utter a word. The dealer looked at me, silently asking if I wanted a hit. I had George scratch the felt on the table meaning we wanted a hit.

The dealer freaked out screaming, **"I'm supposed to deal to a damn monkey?"**

We both nodded and smiled, as the fellow sitting next to me asked her, "Didn't you grow up with Curious George?"

"Nah, I never heard of him."

The dealer got angrier; she called the pit boss over.

Upon arrival he asked in a husky voice, "What seems to be the problem?"

The dealer responded, **"This lady is nuts, she wants me to deal to her monkey!"**

The pit boss took a look at me and George and asked, "What does the monkey have?"

The dealer said: "Fourteen."

George scratched the felt again asking for a hit.

The pit boss said, **"Hit the monkey!"**

The dealer said, "Seven, 21 for the monkey!"

Cheering and clapping arose from the crowd that had gathered, we picked up our winnings and, walked away giggling. After that our evening was quieter, until we hit **our first $100 jackpot....**

Stand-up, Don't run

In 1989 when I was just starting out doing stand-up in San Francisco I got to open at a small dive for Margaret Cho one night.

I was very nervous and had accidentally received caffeinated mocha instead of a decaffeinated mocha. I am allergic to caffeine and spoke so fast that the audience did not understand a word I said.

I was so mortified, I finally asked one member of the audience what was wrong, they said:

"You're talking too fast!"

So I slowed my speech down to a v-e-r-y S-l-l-l-l-l-o-w pace and they finally laughed at me making fun of myself.

It took humiliating myself in front of a crowd of strangers to inspire me to think quickly and save face. On stage sometimes it works, sometimes it doesn't, but it's always worth trying.

Success is often achieved by those who don't know that failure is inevitable.

--Coco Chanel

The Wedding Dance

I went to my brother's wedding, with my partner of two years. We weren't dancing, so Mom took a swig of champagne, walked over to my girlfriend and put her hand out gallantly and said, "Come-on Louise, let's freak everyone out..."
I, of course, got up after a few minutes and walked over claiming to be jealous at which point my mother handed my girlfriend to me saying, "That's the point!"

My brother, not wanting us to stand out, promptly told all his friends to grab someone of the same sex and dance with them so we wouldn't be the only same sex couple on the dance floor. Mom says he was being supportive; regardless, I was entertained by his efforts, we all had a great time, and it created a nice memory.

The power of laughter helped us all deal with a potentially uncomfortable situation.

Or as one of the guests added upon reflection:
When in doubt, grab your partner, swing and shout....

Life's only lasting joy comes in erasing the boundary line between "mine" and "yours"
                                        --Anonymous

The Spirit of Hawaii

When I found my life partner and decided to have a big Jewish wedding, my partner and mother listened to the endless discussions about the invitation list and locations. Eventually I calculated the cost, and made an immediate decision to vote for getting married on the beach alone. My partner was elated. Mom was so supportive she even encouraged my father to pay for the ceremony!

It was going to be a sunrise ceremony on Kauai, *just the two of us.*
When I was talking to my mother about it, she said "Sunrise? Well, that's a little early for your father and me."

(long pause by me)

I said, "You're coming?"
She said, "Of course!"

I was gasping for air, torn between being completely touched and feeling loved, to panicking. Knowing full well they did not like to travel and that this trip was a big deal for them, I rolled with the surprise and said, "Great, we'll have fun."

So my parents came for the ceremony and joined us on our honeymoon!
Think about that for a minute.

You are forgiven for your happiness and your successes only if you generously consent to share them.

--Albert Camus

We saw them every other day for a meal or a Napali coast boat ride, when we took turns getting nauseated, or to swim and save my father from drowning a few times.
(That undertow is mean on Kauai.)

The ceremony was slated for everyone to be there at 5:30 a.m.
I stayed up the first half of the night listening to the pouring rain and wondering whether it would ever stop and what we would do if it didn't. In between the torrential rain and wind were the sounds of roosters talking to each other:
"Cockadoodle doo!" (I am over here)
"Cockadoodle doo!" (well, I am over HERE)
"Cockadoodle doo!" (will you two shut up so I can sleep?)

My partner got up at 4:30 a.m. screaming something about not having enough time to get dressed and look presentable. A few expletives were thrown in.

Did I mention we were having a mild hurricane with buckets of rain all night?

She came out about half an hour later looking **extremely beautiful** and better than I did…
Not funny.

58

We saw lights approach down the dark street at 5:25 a.m. Bless them, it was my parents right on time. The guitarist, and then the photographer followed them; so far it was all going great.

The woman who was to perform the ceremony was a Hawaiian spirit woman, who arrived stoned. We really didn't mind, as she was very sweet and full of good energy.

She explained to us that she would be chanting in Hawaiian and motioning us slowly to walk towards her. The wind was so wildly strong our clothes were blowing off us as we stood watching her sing. We tried to walk towards her a little faster; she motioned us to slow down. She stood in front of my parents who were getting whipped with the fifteen-foot flags we had brought from Portland and set in the sand.

Between the flags, the stoned spirit woman and the red rover dance on the beach, we were in hysterics for the first 20 minutes. Once it was time for my partner to read her vows, my parents couldn't hear because of the wind, so they put their heads right next to hers. She started to laugh as she looked to her left and saw my father's head and on her right my mother's. It was funny and sweet at the same time. She got through her vows beautifully. I, on the other hand was so nervous I blubbered like a baby after the first two words.

The ceremony seemed like a good sign for our future together. Laughter, drama and a supportive loving family; the elements were no match for this potent combination.

Humor is a rich and versatile power- a spiritual resource very like prayer.

--Marilyn Chandler

FIVE

The Fifth Secret

Humor can enrich your relationships and make the unbearable bearable

Animals

Animals can be sensitive, expressive, and loving companions. Observe your animals, they hold the true secrets to letting go of stress.
They also possess the ability to laugh!

You can say any foolish thing to a dog, and the dog will give you a look that says, 'My God, you're right! I never would've thought of that!'
--Dave Barry

Our family grew up with dogs and cats over the years. They were the glue that held the family together during crazy times. We all confided in our animals.
If they could have talked they would have had the first reality television show on cable in the 60's.

An interesting fact about animals is that they are sensitive and can feel your emotions.
How many times have you been fighting with someone in your house, a spouse, friend or foe and the dog or cat hides?

Or better still, the animal comes into the room and tries to get your attention? They are reminding you that fighting is unpleasant and the simple thing to do is pet them and leave whatever problem you are having alone for now.

*All animals except man know that the ultimate
goal of life is to enjoy it.*
> --Samuel Butler

Our pets would prefer that you pet them or feed
them a treat instead of any other activity you have
in mind, especially fighting. It's their nature.
Frankly, I agree with them. I would much rather
be petted and fed a treat than fight.

Some animals still like to find their own treats.

One of the more poignantly funny stories I can
remember about our family's beloved dogs is
about our dog Charlie Brown.
He escaped many times to terrorize the
neighborhood cats. Usually not completing the
chase, he would get distracted by the squirrels and
occasional rabbits in the neighborhood.

This time CB, as we nicknamed him, had been
gone for hours. We combed the neighborhood
and had calls reporting his whereabouts but were
unable to catch him.
He finally showed up at the back door with a poor
unsuspecting wild bunny rabbit that he had
caught. He looked at my mother as if she should
now cook it for him.

He sat there so proud of himself, we had to
laugh and then we had a funeral for the bunny, it
was only proper.

Dearest bunny,
Your life was shortened by our bad dog
He probably found you near the bog
We hope you go to heaven to hop along
Just be glad we didn't try to sing you a song
Amen

Our dogs Desi and Lucy are sisters.
They sleep on top of each other, they chase each
other around the house and they play
with each other all day long.
I try as much as possible to play with them. We
have a little racecourse I set up around the first
floor where I run and they chase me at least once
a day. The hardwood floors are especially fun for
them as they slide around the corners.
I do laps until they stop chasing me or I can't
breathe, whichever comes first.
The best part of this exercise is I laugh the whole
time. It's a great reminder of the joy that kids get
by just running around outside. Just because it's
my aerobic activity for the day doesn't mean it's
any less serious.

This way I exercise by laughing and running!

Dogs laugh, but they laugh with their tails.
                    --Max Eastman

The Mother Puzzle

Here's a story about growing up with two
mothers, and how confusing that can be.
I found a way to laugh about this despite my
frustrations over the years.
After all, I knew how lucky I was to have two
mothers, let alone one.

When I was 15 years old, I went to the local
Barclays Bank to open my first checking account.
I walked right up to the most official looking
person in a suit and told him I wanted to open an
account. He handed me some papers to fill out
and told me to call him over if I had any
questions. I was filling in the blanks:

Name: G-a-i-l. . .
Address: 2-6-6-2 . . .
Phone number: 4-1-5. . .
Mother's Maiden-name: Uh-oh . . .

What was I supposed to put down?
I walked over to the bank officer.
"Why do you need to know my mother's maiden
name?" I pleaded.
"It's the law," he barked.
"What do you mean, it's the law? This is a
ridiculous law. This is **my** account not my
mother's!"
He made it perfectly clear, in no uncertain terms,
that if I wanted an account, I had to put something

down. I finished filling out the paperwork and handed it to him.

"I just wanted to let you know that in the mother's maiden name area I put both my mothers' names down. Look, I even put a slash in between so you wouldn't get confused."

Marks/Martin

"Well, which is it? Marks or Martin? You can only put one."

"I can't just put one. You see I had one mother until I was 11 months old, and then my other mother came along six months later and she raised me, so she is my mother too!"

The bank officer was still not happy with me. He glared back at me waiting for me to make a decision.

I put my late mother's name down and walked out disgusted.

A few months later I walked in to cash a check. The bank teller asked me for my mother's maiden name. I turned white because I could not, for the life of me, remember which name I put down.

"Look, I have two mothers. One raised me until I was 11 months old, and the other raised me since then. So it's one of them. Marks or Martin. Please just cash my check. If someone else can come into the bank and duplicate this story then you can give them all the money in my account."
The woman cashed my check.

You gain strength, courage and confidence by every experience in which you really stop to look fear in the face. You are able to say to yourself,

66

'I've lived through this horror. I can take the next thing that comes along.' You must do the thing you think you cannot do.

--Eleanor Roosevelt

Angels or Horses?

My mother Audrey told me on many occasions that when I traveled she put four white horses around my car to protect me from harm while driving.
Was there something she knew that I didn't?
After all, I was a teenager at the time.

Well, the horses must have gone on to heaven, because the first year I moved to Oregon, I felt like I had a bulls-eye on my car with a sign that read:

Please hit me, I enjoy the stress!

The first one happened in Canada. My partner and I were on vacation, or at least we were trying.

We took off from Portland at 5:30 a.m., arriving in Seattle in time to make the next plane to Calgary. The plane was broken and there was no replacement. We had to wait in the Seattle airport for five hours on my partner's birthday. It was disappointing, but we looked for the humor in it, and found it in a movie.
We rented a DVD player along with an Eddie Murphy comedy and laughed for hours. Later we

got short massages, had our free cafeteria lunches courtesy of Alaska Airlines and boarded the plane.

We sighed with relief as we circled the airport to land in Calgary.

Just as we were approaching, a flock of geese flew into the engine and the plane dropped and swerved. Passengers were yelling, and we sunk down in our seats and looked out the window to see goose feathers everywhere. It was quite a sight.

We all discussed our luck, or lack of it on this flight and analyzed what had happened. The passengers next to me decided that our day was going much better than the driver 500 feet below us who just drove into a group of catapulting geese.
Soon we landed safely and drove to our next destination, Banff.

We arrived at the hotel to find signs posted everywhere informing us that a local resident who had been cross-country skiing on the outskirts of town had been eaten that week by a mountain lion. We decided not to push our luck and avoided cross-country skiing.

We hit the slopes later that day, saw a moose on the side of the road and thought to ourselves that now everything would be great because the moose chose *not* to charge our car.

We took a few runs on the slopes. It was 20
below zero. Cold but beautiful.
After lunch we traversed from one run to the other
on a trail that had been made by other skiers.

There were rocks we could not see until they were
right under our skis. Deb fell up the hill (down
would have been ugly) and I fell right behind her
into a pile of rocks.
She cracked her ski and I hurt my ribs.

We laughed all the way down the mountain at the
vacation antics so far, but we kept going. We
went to town, got the ski fixed, iced my ribs and
hit the mineral baths at the hotel. All was well
with the world.

The next day we had a nice, freezing time skiing
at Lake Louise, but again stumbled over some
rocks. This time we went right into the lodge and
enjoyed the fire. At some point you just shouldn't
push your luck.

We had a day of peace and drove back to Calgary
to return our rental Jeep and catch our plane
home. We talked about seeing downtown
Calgary, as the architecture was supposed to be
interesting. I turned down a main road, got
downtown and saw the buildings.
At this point I had no idea how to get back to the
airport, so I pulled over next to a bus and asked
directions. I often ask myself why the fellow took

so long to explain the directions or why he couldn't have taken longer.

I got in the car and approached a green light and an empty intersection.
As I entered the intersection, a nice young man was running the red light about 50 mph. I did my best to swerve out of the way, as did he, but he skidded into our car.
Happy to be alive, we did the insurance exchange routine and went on our way to catch our plane.

When we arrived home, the house had not burned down, the dog was alive and we considered ourselves lucky.

Today we laugh about the great Canadian vacation, as we did while we were there.

The moral of the story:
When traveling to Canada, buy the rental insurance, watch out for rocks and mountain lions in the snow and take advantage of the exchange rate!

Laughter is the sun that drives winter from the human face.
--Victor Hugo

Six

The Sixth Secret

Laughter can see you through-no matter what circumstances life hands you.

What soap is to the body, laughter is to the soul.
                                    --Yiddish proverb

Choices

My mother was making my Bas Mitzvah dress.
Later she turned to my father and said to him, "*This child is deformed. The dress is three inches longer on one side.*"

During a routine camp physical in 1975, a doctor discovered I had a **severe case of scoliosis** in my spine. After visiting several specialists we determined there were two choices for correction: **One** - Spinal fusion surgery, where the surgeon would **cut up my spine** and take a piece of bone from my hip, chop it up into little pieces, then insert the pieces of bone back between my spinal vertebrae, and finally hook a 12-inch metal rod onto my spine and the spine would fuse itself back together. This healing would happen during the next nine months when I was to wear a body cast. This solution had a 90% chance of correction.
Two- wearing a bulky **skeletal-like metal brace** for three to four years, with about the same percentage of correction. The one positive aspect to this choice was that it was removable and I could shower daily.
As a vain and thoughtful child, **my first concerns were as follows:** How big would the **scar** on my back be? Would I still be able to play sports in the cast?

Would the metal brace **get rusty and squeak** when I walked? Was there a chance of the **rod popping out** at some point?

After they did the surgery, would this make the **metal detector** in airports go off?

After careful debate (25 seconds of crying) I opted for the surgery and the body cast.
DO not pass go, do not collect $200...Instead the Dr. collected $10,000 and I received a **get out of school free card**.

The mummy returns

When I first got the cast on, I came home from the hospital and lay in the front lawn on a lawn chair, getting some sun and drinking water through a straw.
One of the things I remember the most is losing my balance all the time; **I was forever losing my balance in the cast**. The first time I went to school I slipped on a piece of paper and fell flat on my back, the body cast knocking me right out. I came to, only to find people stepping over me to get to their locker. If anyone offered to help me I said I was OK, because I was too embarrassed. Finally the Home-Economics teacher came out to lock the door before class and saw me lying their crying because **I had fallen and could not get up**. She helped me up and then walked me to class because she wanted to explain to the other teacher what had happened and why I was late.

Once we got to German class I looked through the door at several of my friends who I had not seen since 8th grade. Thanking my savior, I turned to see **30 pairs of eyes on me**. The teacher told me there was a seat in the back of the room.

I knew this was not a good place for me to stretch my legs but I went and sat there anyway. As I walked into the class alone, I felt like I had to walk nine miles with the whole class observing my every move. **I was concentrating so hard on not tripping and getting the gazing eyes off of me**.... that when I finally reached my chair in the back of the room, I clumsily plunked myself down and proceeded to lean back too quickly. My cast knocked very loudly against the blackboard behind me and made a **very loud noise**. This threw the teacher off and SHE tripped and **her papers flew all over the room.** The whole class laughed at her including me and thus started my freshman year of high school.

The experience was difficult and funny at the same time. I made a concerned effort to always try and find the humor to get through that difficult year. Dwelling on the anger I felt as a teenager in a body cast wasn't going to make the year move along any faster.

To most people, I was a zombie-like creature who walked into a room to an eyeful of stares, all of them wondering what had happened to me and if it was going to scar me permanently.
Day after day I would tire of explaining my surgery to people over and over again.

Most people would not have the courage to talk to me let alone ask what happened to me.
However, one day I was trapped on an elevator with a woman in the building where my parents worked.

The woman stared at me for a few seconds and then said: **What on earth happened to you?** I was in a playful mood, so I told her, "my family was on a picture safari in Kenya, and I was trampled by an elephant". Then the elevator door opened at my parents' floor, so I turned to her smiling and said: "Have a nice day."

She was still reacting from the story as the doors closed yelling "You take care of yourself young lady."
I was **hysterically laughing** by the time I reached my parents' office and my mother knew I was up to no good by the look on my face and the hysteria with which I presented myself. She said, "What are you laughing so hard for, what trouble did you get yourself into?" My mother has a great sense of humor, so I told her the story. **To my surprise she scolded me and told me I was going to go to hell.** I looked at her quizzically and said: **"You mean this isn't it?"**

It was quite a cast I wore, it **held my head erect** so that I could not turn around to see what was behind me unless I turned my whole entire body around, which took a long time sometimes. SO **twisting was out**.
Of course the kids at school figured out this was their best chance at **teasing** me relentlessly. I

would sit in the front seat of class so that I could stretch my legs because the circulation would get cut off in my body cast on my legs. So **the kids behind me would call my name** and I would take what seemed like a whole minute to turn around to see what they wanted from me and big surprise no one would fess up to having called me. This would continue until I got so tired of turning around I would get mad and try to turn just my neck which I then would **wrench into the plaster** Oh that was of great pleasure to the kids who teased me. They had got me to hurt myself! Talk about cruel. No wonder it's taken me 20 years to write about it. I got my first taste of dark humor.

What seems to us bitter trials are often blessings in disguise
  --Oscar Wilde

Teenagers

My neighbor and I had a bimonthly appointment for him to check to make sure everything was still growing and not being squished by the cast. **One time my mom got home early from work and almost caught us.** Billy was in a rush to get his hand out of my cast and for a joke I moved my chest forward which caused his hand to get **stuck in the cast**, giving him a **real scare.** (sort of like getting your hand stuck in the cookie jar) I told him if he didn't stop taking so long he would lose his privileges.

Recreation

Over the Christmas holiday my family went up to go skiing in Lake Tahoe. In fact we rented a nice cabin across from Heavenly Valley that we stayed in.

I came fully prepared to go skiing with my skis, boots and the rest. **There was some discussion as to whether or not it was a good idea for me to ski, as I had no peripheral vision.** I had been skiing since I was three years old, so I was not about to let a body cast and restricted vision get in my way of playing in the snow. After all, as a lifelong skier I was so confident there was no negotiation necessary. My father brought up his biggest concern. **What if she falls?**

I said **"Dad, if I fall I will just fly down the hill on my face faster than other skiers because I will be catapulted by the flat plaster on the snow! You can ski with me and help me up. Then I will go inside and have some hot chocolate like I usually do after I take a good fall!"**

Everyone kind of chuckled at the thought of me as a human sled and off we went to ski. I took it easy for a few runs and then started to lose my balance on one run. I fell face-first, my ski's locked behind my head, flying down the hill.

Naturally my father was 30 yards below me when I finally stopped. I yelled, **"Help! I've fallen and I can't get up"**... My dad looked up at me and sighed, "Are you hurt?" **"I don't think so but I can't get up by myself!"** My dad slowly started stepping up the hill to me. A few minutes later a nice man yelled from the chairlift asking if I needed help. I said, **"Yes I do!"** (Knowing that he could get to me faster than my father, as I was not exactly comfortable in this position) **About a minute later he skied right next to me swishing a blast of snow in my face;** this I remember very well. This nice man helped me up and helped dust me off. When he felt the hard body cast as he helped me up, he said; "Do you have a cast on"? I admitted that I did and he couldn't believe that I was skiing. **I just laughed and said I needed an adventure that day.**

My father eventually arrived and the two of them helped me get my skis back on. It took both of them because I kept losing my balance. Dad followed me to the lodge and this time helped me get my skis off as I was a bit shaken up. In we walked to meet my mother for a good laugh and some hot chocolate.

She took one look at the remaining snow on my body and the look on my face and said,

"Are you happy now? Are you happy now?"

When you know you are doing the very best within the circumstances of your existence, applaud yourself!

--Rusty Berkus

Then there was the time I went skateboarding…

Accidents

Car Karma

One bright spring day I was driving down Highway 580 in the Bay Area, better known at the time as the MacArthur Freeway. I was rounding the corner to merge onto Highway 80 at Emeryville near the San Pablo entrance. Up from the on-ramp came a woman going about 60 mph, who decided to merge into the traffic which had slowed down to about 40 mph.

We proceeded to merge into the same lane, and she crossed over the solid white line. To avoid colliding with her, I veered to the left **hard.** My Jeep spun around 180 degrees, which meant I was now driving into five lanes of **oncoming** traffic. I dodged a few cars and started to laugh. I yelled out loud:

"Hey this is great, is this how I'm going to go?"

Suddenly, after the fourth car whizzed by mine in the opposite direction, the five lanes of traffic stopped to a dead halt. The driver I was face to face with motioned me to turn around. I tried to start my car, which was, of course, already running.

In the end I was fine, the other car totaled and the passengers relatively unscathed.

Sometimes we have a chance to meet danger
head-on and laugh, Just remember if it happens
*to you in a car as it did to me, steer **into** the skid.*

Errands

I live in Northeast Portland, a wonderful place
with shops and neighborhoods that give you the
feeling you are in a small village.

That day I had been out running errands and I
remember saying to myself at the red light as I
was leaving the shopping center,
"You can do this last one tomorrow--don't push
yourself--it's raining and people don't drive as
well in the rain--just go home and rest--you're
tired."
Did I listen? No, of course not.
I pulled onto Broadway and drove ten blocks
down to the alterations store where I proceeded to
park.
As I sat there, I watched another driver back into
my car. I honked and waved at him, but it was too
late. He refused to claim responsibility, and then
managed to pay off five witnesses to lie to my
insurance company. I had to pay a $500
deductible and my car had $3,000 worth of
damage. My insurance went to court and lost!

All this because I wanted to do an extra errand!

You would think that perhaps that was the end of
my bad car karma. Think again!

The next month a nice uninsured motorist ran a red light and *totaled* my newly repaired car.

It was as if the universe was saying, you think this is bad? **Take that!**

The reward of suffering is experience.
                              --Aeschylus

It took me a long time to laugh about it, a year to drive by the alterations store and not make rude gestures at their window, and seven months to recover from the second accident.
I drove a lot less and wrote in my journal often.

After we get through the anger and the sadness that the events bring, it is possible to laugh at the little details.
For instance, as a result I ended up financially in a better position because my car lease ended three months after the accident.

Overall I felt pretty fortunate and took my jolly sweet time buying a new car, thanks to my partner. I lived through three accidents in three months and lived to tell the tales.
For this I am thankful and pause before a green lighted intersection on a regular basis and smile if someone honks to rush me.

Emotions are emotions, I believe in having them, dealing with them and moving on.
It can take a long time with some events but it is possible to move on to the next adventure.

So many things we do in our lives start with what goes on in our minds. I am driven to figure out how to teach others to look at a situation in a humorous manner when appropriate, so that they can get through that time easier.

Change your thoughts and you change your world.

--Norman Vincent Peale

Living every day we have to deal with fear from the past, present or future. Many people cannot progress because they hold onto a lousy experience. This fear keeps them from growing.

Finding the humor in a dark situation takes courage. *Why?* Because you need to look beyond the lack of control you have in this situation and make a choice to become stronger that moment. By doing this you create a positive effect from a negative beginning. It's all up to you.

Why hold on to something that has passed?
As a wise therapist once advised me, slay the dragon with your courage, kill it; or don't kill it, just look it in the eyes and say, "Enough!"
When it came time for me to slay my own dragon, I decided I would not kill it, but tickle it under its long neck and make a friend. You never know when you may need a dragon to help you along your path.

Seven

The Seventh Secret

Learning to cope with death is good for your mental health, and laughter can ease the pain.

Death, taxes and childbirth! There's never any
convenient time for any of them.

       --Margaret Mitchell

The appropriateness of laughter

How can I laugh when a relative just passed away,
or at something as difficult as the Holocaust?

This is an excerpt from a doctoral thesis
submitted to Tel Aviv University
Entitled: "Humor as a Defense mechanism in
the Holocaust"

The author demonstrated on the basis of extensive
interviews with survivors that even with a
horribly stressful situation like the Holocaust,
humor was a stress reducer and enabled victims to
survive a bit longer.

The use of humor during the Holocaust did not
reduce the objective atrocity or horror, rather it
reduced them subjectively, and facilitated coping
with them.
Humor was expressed in different modes during
the Holocaust. In addition to humorous
utterances and episode interpretations, there were
also humorous songs, humorous reviews and
cabarets and caricature painting and drawings.

One survivor said to Octrower: "Without humor we would all have committed suicide. We made fun of everything. What I'm actually saying is that laughter helped us remain human, even under hard conditions...I don't think that it is possible for people in such situations not to have any humor and satire. This is impossible, it is kind of defense mechanism.. At the Ghetto we were looking underground for things to laugh at, even if there weren't any."

This research reminds us of the recent comedic movie "Life is Beautiful," a movie about the Holocaust. To many the idea is perverse, in poor taste. Yet, as the film develops, it is clear that Roberto Benigni, the writer, director, and lead actor created a powerful film that manages to entertain, educate, and inspire with its potent combination of poignancy and dignity framed in laughter!

Now you can see by example the power of the human spirit. I too, had relatives who perished in the Holocaust. It never occurred to me, even as a stand-up comedian, that there would **ever** be anything remotely funny about the Holocaust. Yet this research shows that laughter was not only used as a survival tool for the prisoners daily coping but helped increase their emotional well-being, increasing their chances for survival.

In the depth of winter, I finally learned that within me there lay an invincible summer.
                                                    --Albert Camus

New York

9/11 was horrible for all of us. It reminded us of the sanctity of life, the gift of freedom we cherish in our great nation, and that any day can be our last.

Like many people, every time I hear about a plane crash, I hope it has nothing to do with terrorism. I have had several good friends die in the past few years and it always hits me that our days are numbered and our choices need to be clear. We need to choose to look at the events in our lives from a different angle sometimes in order to cope with the atrocities.

One day in retrospect the years of struggle will strike you as the most beautiful.
                                                    --Sigmund Freud

My fondest memory of the World Trade Center was lying on the concrete below the buildings with my best friend Nancy without a dime in our pockets, laughing as they moved in the wind.

I always knew I would look back at the times I'd cried, and laugh, but I never knew that I'd look back at the times I'd laughed and cry.
                                                    --Shaun Prowdzik

Many people fear death, some embrace it because they have no choice, others simply don't want to talk about it.

I relate to this topic on several levels. The first is that I lost my mother to cancer when I was 11 months old. She was 31 and we barely knew each other. Right after my mother died, her mother fell ill of another form of cancer and died three months later. You may be thinking, what was the third thing, as great proverbs tell us bad things happen in threes.

It just so happens that three months after my Grandmother died, my grandfather rear- ended someone in a routine traffic accident. He was fine, got out of his car to see if everyone was okay in the other car and then he dropped dead of a heart attack as he reached his car.

My whole life I heard this story told in so many different ways. My second mother, Audrey tells it best, as she attended two of the three funerals. She also explains to others why it's not possible that I look like her because she is not my real mother, that my real mother died when I was a toddler, and so on.

It took me so many years to figure out the parameters of the severity of the whole situation. Every year as it got close to my mother's anniversary date of her diagnoses and hospitalization, I would get sick. Then I would get depressed.

It took me ten years with a good therapist to figure it out after my own illnesses were more and more noticeable. Once I realized why I was getting sick, suddenly it just stopped. I thought that was kind of funny. Others didn't, but I was a dark-humored kid.

When the same thing happened after my Grandmother died, I realized that I had better get a handle on my feelings before it killed me. Better yet, find a way to **celebrate her life** .

The statistics on sanity are that one out of every four Americans is suffering from some form of mental illness. Think of your three best friends. If they are okay, then it's you.
--Rita Mae Brown

My mother's death anniversary is around Labor Day. This holiday is a time that people go away on camping trips or visit their families. If I go camping, I'll do silly things that make me happy, like eating s'mores, get them all over my face and take pictures.

I have a friend whose mother died around the same time of year. She goes to the beach and eats Oreos. Both of us remind ourselves to honor our mothers, and celebrate the moments of our youth and laugh.

I like living. I have sometimes been wildly, despairingly, acutely miserable, racked with sorrow, but through it all I still know quite certainly that just to be alive is a grand thing.
--Agatha Christie

Dark Comedy

An important aspect of humor is to know when not to make light of things that are serious. When is it just inappropriate to make jokes?

In today's world of dark comedy, which has been around since before we were all here, there are things that are still not politically correct to joke about. Yet there are comics that go to that place over the edge often, and we admire them for their courage.

Courageous is just about the right thing to call their work. Not all of us have the inclination to let our egos get out of the way long enough to enjoy this type of humor.

A recent special on cable TV by George Carlin is a good example. If you are courageous enough to listen to his whole show, you'll realize that he is truly concerned about the issues he makes light of; you just have to give him a chance to finish the whole bit.

Carlin is an expert at dealing with irony.

Dark humor is one of the best ways to deal with a tough situation because it helps us get to the core of the situation.

A gifted comedian using wry humor with difficult subjects can help us stay on track with our feelings, a form of therapy for which we could be grateful.

All of us try so hard to understand death, and yet how can we understand it when we haven't experienced it? It's like a sport you have never played, but only watched.

Life is pleasant. Death is peaceful. It's the transition that's troublesome.
                                                    --Isaac Asimov

Many people make light of death because they don't understand it. We all try to find comfort in our grief with fond memories hopefully getting in touch with our chosen spirituality for added comfort and understanding.

Ancient Egyptians believed that upon death they would be asked two questions and their answers would determine whether they could continue their journey in the afterlife. The first question was, "Did you bring joy?" The second was, "Did you find joy?"
                                                    --Leo Buscaglia

Brass Tacks and Whoopee Cushions

So now what? How do I change my life through adding more laughter?

In today's changing world just getting through the day can be a struggle for some of us. We all have a choice to meet the world's demands with a good attitude and a sense of humor.

Laughter is a gift you can give to other people,

If you humiliate yourself in the process, even better!

Here are some ideas that other comedians, humorists, speakers and people not afraid to let go-do.

Buy a fun costume, wear it somewhere public and greet people as they arrive. Recently over the holidays I wore a Winnie the Pooh outfit and greeted my relatives and 100 other strangers in the arrival area of the airport. (Pick another location, security is tough enough these days without needing to deal with adults in drag.)

Find a clown nose or the classic glasses and rubber nose. Put them on at a stoplight and wave to your neighbor, or better yet don't –just stare.

Approach the person at the airport baggage claim holding the sign without your name on it. Strike up a nice conversation until the real person comes along. This is best done if your baggage is late and you have nothing else to do.

Take a break during your day to enjoy humor. You may do this by reading the funnies, reading a comical book you picked up from the library or choosing one of the humor sites listed below.

Your HR group should approve all of these sites as you are helping your mental health by taking a humor break.

In addition, your productivity will improve, your attitude will shine and you will get that much sought after promotion! If you are working at home, you may want to water your plants or walk the dog for improved productivity at home.

This break will stir your creativity and give you mind a few minutes to relax.

In the end the choice is yours, I choose to laugh.

Bibliography

Carlson, Richard, PhD., *Don't Sweat the Small Stuff at Work*. New York, Hyperion, 1998.

Weiss, Rabbi Avi, *Isaac's Legacy for survival* Jewish Community Journal, 2000.

Moore, Mike, *The Healing Power of Laughter*. Self Improvement Online, Inc., 1999.

Cousins, Norman, *Anatomy of an Illness*. New York, W.W. Norton, 1979.

Fry, Dr. William, *The Healing Effects of Humor*. American Medical Association, 1992.

Ostrower, Chaya, *Humor as a defense Mechanism in the Holocaust*. Tel Aviv University, 2000.

Kimata, Hajime, MD, PhD, *The Healing Power of Humor, Laughter May be the Best Medicine for Hives*.
Journal of American Medical Association, 2001.

Laughter Tools

Recommended Web Sites

www.thelaughweb.com

Movie Reviews, CD's, DVD's and Cartoons
Available in seven languages!

www.humorproject.com

Dr. Joel Goodman, author and entrepreneur
started this project in Saratoga, NY to spread
the word of laughter to the world.
The bookstore has many good selections.

www.flighthumor.org

The University of Dayton's flight humor contest
has picked the funniest, true stories about flying.

www.intercall.com/~mayz/lh.htm

The Laurel and Hardy - Wonders of Comedy site
offers information and trivia about the comedy
duo. The site includes short biographies of the
comedians, a filmography, a television listing and
links to other classic film pages.

www.laughter.org

Their goal is to provide the ultimate source of comedy information the web Laughter Dot Org will feature news and reviews of comedy albums, books, movies, television shows, performers, and web sites..

www.netlaughter.com

Funny pictures, videos, movies, email forwards, downloads, and jokes

www.laughter.com

Funny pictures, videos, movies, email forwards, downloads, and jokes

www.aath.org

Association for Applied Theraputic Humor Therapeutic humor resources and articles. Develops and supports research into the use of humor

www.learnimprov.com
This simple site is devoted to learning improvisational comedy. One cannot really learn improvisational comedy from a web page, however the list of exercises included here will definitely help

Recommended Reading to instill more laughter and peace in your life

All Allen Klein's Books

Anatomy of An Illness, Norman Cousins

Larry Wilde's Official joke books

Laughter: A Scientific Investigation, R. R. Provine

Laughter Therapy, Karen Mueller Bryson

Shiksa Goddess, Wendy Wasserstein

10 secrets for success and inner peace, Dr. W Dyer

Fractured Fairy Tales, A.J. Jacobs

The Healing Power of Humor, Bernie Siegel

What would Buddha Do?, Franz Metcalf

How to be Happy, dammit. Karen Salmansohn

Dave Barry's Books and Columns

The gift of laughter-6-hour audio cassette, Patricia Fripp with Larry Wilde

Improvise This!, Mark Bergren, Molly Cox & Jim Detmar

301 Ways to Have Fun at Work, Dave Hemsath & Leslie Yerkes

The Healing Power of the Hawaiian-Style Belly Laugh, Pat Masumoto

DVD/Videos you may rent for a nice laughter break

Classics video collections:
Abbott & Costello
Marx Brothers
Three Stooges
Laurel & Hardy
Fellini-All

British Humor
Monty Python-any
Mr. Bean – any
Benny Hill- any (naughty)
Tracey Ullman

Movies Titles:
A Fish called Wanda
American Pie I & II
Analyze This
Arthur
Austin Powers Series
Better off Dead
Bill Cosby, Himself
Billy Madison
Blazing Saddles
Bridget Jones Diary
Bullets over Broadway
Bullworth
Caddyshack
City Slickers 1 & 2
Defending Your Life
Dr. Strangelove
Fargo
Ferris Buellers Day Off
Fletch
Foul Play
Ghostbusters

Gross Pt. Blank
Groundhog Day
Hairspray
Happy Gilmore
Harold & Maude
History of the World
Home Alone
Home for the Holidays
It's a Mad, Mad, Mad, Mad World
Kissing Jessica Stein
Meet the Parents
Midnight Run
Mrs. Doubtfire
My Big Fat Greek Wedding
National Lampoon's Vacation
Never been kissed
9 to 5
Postcards from the Edge
Princess Bride
Priscilla Queen of the Desert
Saving Grace
Shrek
Sister Act I & II
Sixteen Candles
Sleeper
Spaceballs
Steel Magnolias
Stripes
The Big Lebowski
The Full Monty
The Jerk
The Kings of Comedy
The Royal Tannenbaum's
There's Something About Mary
The Wedding Singer
What about Bob?
Young Frankenstein

Comedians, the Aristotle's of the 00's

There are many great comedians in the world, who are wonderful at finding the irony in life; it's their job.

If you don't have the comedy channel on cable go to your local video store and look for these to start:

Jack Benny, Milton Berle, Elayne Boosler, Carol Burnett, George Burns, Drew Carey, George Carlin, Dana Carvey, Margaret Cho, Kate Clinton, Bill Cosby, Billy Crystal, Phyllis Diller, Ellen Degeneres, Whoopie Goldberg, Bob Hope, Cathy Ladman, Dennis Leary, Jay Leno, David Letterman, Graham Norton, Paula Poundstone, Paul Reiser, Chris Rock, Rita Rudner, Adam Sandler, Jerry Seinfeld, Danny Thomas, Robin Williams, Tracey Ullman, and Steven Wright.

Funny Basic Channels TV Shows:

The Ellen Degeneres Show (New in Fall 2003)
Ellen at her best with funny monologues you would usually have to pay to see. She's bringing dancing, napping and glamour back to daytime.

Frasier
Great writing, always a lot of fun

Everybody Loves Raymond
Everyone loves to laugh, these Emmy awards winning Actors will keep you in stitches.

Will & Grace
Simply fabulous and very funny.

For those of you who have cable:

The Tracey Ullman Show
In my opinion the best character actress other than
Carol Burnett ever.

Six Feet Under
Dark Humor- Excellent writing, great show.
(rent the videos if you don't have cable)

South Park
For those with a non-pc iron stomach.
(PG-21 with an open mind-rating)

Nickelodeon
Any old sitcom you turn on will be entertaining.
My faves: Taxi, Addams Family, Andy Griffith,
The Simpsons, Bewitched, Dick Van Dyke, The
Mary Tyler Moore Show, Batman, and many
many others...